TIHANY

Iconic Hotel and Restaurant Interiors

Introduction by Thomas Keller

Prologue by Adam D. Tihany

RIZZOLI
NEW YORK

New York · Paris · London · Milan

To my mother, Judith

First published in the United States of America in 2014 by
Rizzoli International Publications, Inc.
300 Park Avenue South
New York, NY 10010
www.rizzoliusa.com

ISBN: 978-0-8478-4250-6
LCCN: 2013950712

Introduction © 2014 Thomas Keller

Designed by Mirko Ilić Corp., NY

Distributed to the U.S. trade by Random House, New York

Printed and bound in China

2014 2015 2016 2017 2018 / 10 9 8 7 6 5 4 3 2 1

P. 1 **Beverly Hills Hotel – Front Desk.** Photo by Karyn Millet. Pp. 2–3 **Beverly Hills Hotel – Lobby.** Photo by Karyn Millet. Pp. 4–5 **Beverly Hills Hotel – Pool.** Photo by Eric Laignel. Pp. 6–7 **The Joule Hotel, Dallas – Lobby.** Photo by Eric Laignel. Pp. 8 **The Joule Hotel, Dallas – Pool.** Photo by Eric Laignel. Pp. 10–11 **The Joule Hotel, Dallas – Charlie Palmer Restaurant.** Photo by Eric Laignel. Pp. 12–13 **Sirio, New York City – Bar.** Photo by Eric Laignel. Pp. 14–15 **Aria Hotel, City Center Las Vegas – Union Restaurant.** Photo by Eric Laignel. Pp. 16–19 **Bouchon, Beverly Hills – Detail.** Photo by Art Gray.

TABLE OF CONTENTS

INTRODUCTION

BY THOMAS KELLER

For all the credit heaped on restaurant chefs these days, fairly little praise goes to restaurant designers. Call it an injustice of the modern age. Great restaurants, after all, aren't just about great cooking. The best of them have distinctive aesthetics, vivid personalities that make themselves apparent not only in the composition of the menu but in every detail of the dining room. Deciding on those details is the work of the designer, and it isn't easy. It calls for a trained eye, a creative mind, and a special gift for collaboration.

Which is my way of saying that I owe a debt of gratitude to Adam Tihany.

I first met Adam in 1986, when I attended one of his restaurant seminars in New York City. I was beginning to think about designing my first restaurant and was so intrigued by Adam's ideas that I walked up and introduced myself. I was drawn to design and eager to discuss it, but I lacked the vocabulary to talk about it. Adam didn't. I recall him speaking about the wide-ranging roles different materials could play, and the way that light created energy, which, as a young chef, I found fascinating. Talking to Adam was the best introduction anyone could have to what restaurant design is all about.

I didn't know it at the time, but it was also the start of a beautiful friendship and professional partnership.

In the years since, Adam has been central to a number of my projects. Bouchon Bistro in Yountville was the first. Opening that restaurant was a giant step for me, and I needed Adam's help with it. I knew that he could handle anything, from a down-home bistro to a high-concept restaurant. More important, I was certain he could bring my vision for Bouchon to life.

What makes Adam extraordinary is his ability to translate a chef's concept into a reality without having his own ego get in the way. Our work on Bouchon was truly collaborative and together we respected the well-established design of a classic bistro. Yet Adam gave me free reign to express my need to be true to bistro architecture, and he guided me along the way, helping me transform my abstract ambition into a restaurant with a vivid sense of place. Using his vast knowledge of bistro history, he helped me create an urban bistro that referenced the great bistros of the world. The result was something we could both embrace.

An even greater test of our relationship came a few years later when we got to work opening Per Se. At the outset, Adam's first question was: "What kind of feel do you want this restaurant to have?" My response came easily: I directed Adam to create a timeless restaurant, something that in twenty-five years would be just as beautiful as it is today, like The Four Seasons, which is still one of the best examples of contemporary restaurant design. I wanted that same meditative sense of classic luxury. While my directions were straightforward, to the point, it was all easier said than done. As the project unfolded, Adam and Laura Cunningham guided my ideas. Both knew that I wanted a sense of luxury, but a sense of luxury unbound by generations.

Adam understood that I wanted Per Se to be an urban version of French Laundry hospitality, but not just The French Laundry relocated in Manhattan. Those were just my thoughts. Adam helped me turn them into action. At Per Se, we honor The French Laundry with distinctive design touches—the blue door, for instance, remains the same, but instead of a fieldstone entrance, we chose natural stone. Front and center, in the window wall overlooking Central Park, is a wood-burning fireplace, a traditional symbol of hospitality that translates well on either coast. It is, I think, a very beautiful restaurant, but it wouldn't be what it is without Adam. In the course of three years of intense collaboration, he helped me turn my unformed vision into the twenty-first-century luxury restaurant that Per Se is today.

Over the years, Adam has taught me to think of restaurants in a deeper way. I don't just ask myself: What kind of place do I want to open? Nowadays, the questions verge on existential. I ask: Who am I? Where am I coming from? And where, exactly, do I want to go?

The answer to that last question has shifted over time. But no matter where I go next, I can only hope that Adam will go with me. There's a dance people do in long-term relationships and Adam and I have found our rhythm. We know each other's skills, understand each other's needs, and interpret each other's visions. As Thoreau said, "It's not what you look at that matters, it's what you see." Adam Tihany not only sees the world in design, he sees it better than anyone else.

PROLOGUE

BY ADAM D. TIHANY

In 1996, the ebullient Tuscan restaurateur, Sirio Maccioni presented me with the challenge of moving Le Cirque, the hyper-successful, four-star classic into the landmarked 1884 Villard Houses on Madison Avenue. Landmarked meant we literally could not touch one inch of the interior space; we could put not one screw in a wall. My solution was to pitch a tent inside the space and give Sirio, the consummate ringmaster, a true circus: wildly colorful and exciting, a bit shocking, over the top.

At the very same time, just across town on Central Park West, a completely different project was underway: Jean-Georges Vongerichten is a very modern Alsatian genius, a Prada-wearing chef who creates beautiful food. He hired us to design a restaurant that took him back to his roots as a four-star chef. Jean-Georges's restaurant was elegant, luxurious, creamy, minimal, set in a simple glass and metal box in a beautiful location with abundant daylight.

When these two restaurants opened within months of each other, it was difficult for people to believe that the same designer did both of them. And I think that's the best description of Tihany style: I have no one style.

I do portraits. And when I do a portrait of somebody, I put my all my feelings into the way I see it. But the portrait always portrays them, it is never about me. Or, think of me as a custom tailor. If I do a custom suit for Thomas Keller, it will fit him. And it's not the same suit that will fit Daniel Boulud or Jean-Georges. Why would they all hire the same guy? Thomas Keller doesn't want his restaurant to look like Daniel Boulud's. Daniel Boulud doesn't want his restaurant to look like Wolfgang Puck's, or Heston Blumenthal's, or Pierre Gagnaire's. Pierre Gagnaire doesn't want his restaurant to look like Sirio's. And Sirio doesn't want his restaurant to look like anyone else's. That's why they all come to me.

ON BEING ITALIAN

Of course I am not Italian. Or maybe just a little bit. I was born in Transylvania, my ancestors are Romanian, and I grew up speaking Hungarian at home in Jerusalem. Two days after I finished my military service in Israel, I was on a plane to Milan to study architecture.

The years I spent as a working student in Italy—the late '60s into the '70s—the country was not in its brightest moment. Architects and design offices were struggling to find work. There were no major building projects, the economy was not great, so people became resourceful. They adapted. They took on side projects to stay busy, discovering that what matters is the essence and the energy of the product, the importance of detail, whether you're designing a fork or a building. That was how I was brought up in Italian design. No challenge was too big or too small. There was just the problem. Our job was to look for a solution.

For example, if someone had the good fortune to design a new piece of furniture, he would design the packaging and the graphics and the advertising, too. Everything that went into that piece of furniture became interesting. Designers did it because they needed the work, but the end result was that the product became stronger and stronger because you could control every phase of it. That was my formation, the way I studied and learned in the early years. And it turned out to be the perfect foundation for the hospitality designer I was to become, intrigued by designing everything from the plates to the interiors, lighting, fabrics, furniture, and the architecture, too.

This was my biggest conflict when I came to this country, because in my mind I was an Italian designer. People would ask me: What do you design? And I would say: What do you have? Tell me the problem, I'll give you a solution. What are you, they'd ask: an interior designer, an architect, a product designer, a graphic designer, a fashion designer? You can't be all of these things. The American idea is that if you can do more than one thing, you are not an expert in the field. If you were known for Helvetica, that's all you did. You'd get boxed into a specialty so early that I saw that my life was going to end very quickly because I would be doing a chair all my life. This would be my legacy: I designed one great chair, now all I do is chairs. I kept fighting to define myself as more than just one kind of designer. For me, the definition of designer was the Italian definition.

I could never reconcile the fact that to be successful in America I would have to give up a lot of things I like to do and focus on just one aspect of design. I never deliberately

thought: I want to create a profession that allows me to touch all these disciplines. It just fell into my lap!

And it works because I'm a problem solver; that's my whole upbringing, my education. Everything I've done all my life is to confront challenges. I get excited when there is a problem. It becomes almost like a drug, an aphrodisiac. I don't get discouraged. On the contrary, this is what wakes me up in the morning. I think, "Let me go look for a problem." Because if everything was easy, I would miss the adrenaline that comes from facing issues and solving problems. That's what kicks off my creativity.

LA COUPOLE CHANGED EVERYTHING

One day, people from a large New York-based interior design firm looking to bring Italian flair to America visited the design office where I worked in Milan and asked: "Does anybody want to go to America?" I volunteered immediately; I had my suitcase under my chair! I just left everything and came here. America? Of course! That was my dream! I spoke the language: Like every Israeli kid, I grew up on Alfred E. Neuman and *MAD* Magazine and Hugh Hefner and *Playboy*. They were my icons. And of course the streets were paved with gold.

From my first day in New York I felt extremely at ease. This to me was home, an immigrant city like Jerusalem. Everybody is a stranger—and no one is a stranger—with

people speaking seven languages in the street. It was very comforting and familiar. I remember the first moment the taxi drove from the airport into the canyons of Manhattan, I felt my chest opening: Ahhhhh. I suddenly knew: This is it! I am home. The architecture completely blew me away. The whole idea of seeing the sky framed through all of these buildings and the openings to the river. I had never experienced anything like it. It just felt right.

I struggled for the first five years of my American existence as a designer, doing what I could do: an apartment for a friend here, a little shop for a friend there. A small office. I designed the first New York showroom for Gianni Versace. In those early years, Italians were coming to the city and starting businesses, but Italian businessmen were very suspicious of the Americans. They didn't get the culture, so I became the go-between, the Israeli, the bridge. I'd say Okay, you guys deal with me, I'll deal with the Americans! That gave birth to a whole variety of little projects, most of them with Italian flavor.

And then on one of those nights at Xenon (which I designed) or another of the European nightclubs that we frequented at the time, a gentleman with a French accent asked me casually if I wanted to design a restaurant. "Listen," I said, "I would design anything, I'm starving!" I didn't know much about a restaurant except that it was a place to eat.

This was 1980, and as fate had it, the project was called La Coupole.[1] The owner, Jean Denoyer, had the license to re-create the legendary Parisian café La Coupole, which

had opened in 1927 on the Boulevard Montparnasse. So I embarked on a research journey to Paris and examined every detail of the original. Jean and his partners were very trusting. I designed what turned out to be the first grand café in New York City. I did the interiors, I designed the furniture, the uniforms, I selected the graphics, everything. I was Italian! I made the discovery that in this microcosm of restaurant design, I could have my way: I could touch every discipline of the profession that I love doing. It was a revelation that you can do all this in the contained space of one restaurant. La Coupole changed everything for me. The restaurant opened to rave reviews and became an instant hit. I ordered a sign that read: Adam D. Tihany – Restaurant Designer, and hung it outside my studio door.

RESTAURANT DESIGN AS A CAREER?

La Coupole was validation that there could be a niche in this world to encompass every design discipline that I enjoyed. That niche would be called hospitality design and I became the first practitioner. But my true aha moment was to come later, with the story of Remi, which was when restaurant design became a passion, not just a profession.

After La Coupole, hanging out with this social crowd, I became one of them. They trusted me and I was their go-to guy. The early '80s in New York was all

3

4

about Eurostyle nightclubs, exclusive places like Regine that were the anti-Studio 54. No longer was it about being in a loud, cavernous black theater; now it was about getting dressed up and spending the evening with people who enjoyed good Champagne and good service. A Brazilian, Ricardo Amaral, owner of the famous Hippopotamus in Rio de Janeiro, which was the South American nightspot, asked me to design what I think was one of the more beautiful and successful places at the time. Club A[2] was a glamorous nightclub attached to a really superb restaurant, Tucano,[3] an early celebrity-chef-operated place whose chef was Jacques Maximin from Le Chantecler at the Negresco in Nice.

Tucano's design was really a Brazilian concept, very fun and fancy—the whole idea was you'd have drinks, a fantastic dinner, then you'd dance it off the whole night long. We custom-designed everything: furniture, china, glassware, lighting. The restaurant was quite formal and opulent with magnificent, gleaming wood, but full of personality, theme-ish, with toucans everywhere and giant Venetian glass-fruit wall sconces. It fulfilled my ambition and continued my trajectory from La Coupole. So I was still Italian.

Then came DDL Foodshow.[4] DDL is Dino De Laurentiis. Foodshow was the key word, because it was show business, an Italian gourmet grocery store where you'd come in the morning for a cappuccino and stay to buy food for dinner. Places like that did not yet exist in New York. It was an early version of Eataly. Dino was a great

visionary, the big producer who made films at Cinecittà Studios in Rome and pretty much invented the concept of paparazzi, of starlets, of everything great that came from the Italian movie producers of that era. I knew that somehow movie magic had to be part of this incredible store. We met and really hit it off. He found me simpatico. He thought I was Italian.

I wasn't a foodie yet, but I had an inclination. I also realized that I couldn't do this well unless I understood the product, which was the food itself. I needed to see great markets, so I went to Fauchon in Paris, I went to Peck, in Milano (probably for the first time, because I couldn't afford it when I was a student). And Dino was so right. He was a total pioneer completely ahead of his time. When you look at the stores that we created together in New York and Los Angeles—to open a 20,000-square-foot upscale Italian grocery with an Italian espresso bar with rotisserie and live fire on the Upper West Side in 1983? Madness, right? Right?

There were some amazing benefits of that project, and chief among them was meeting Francesco Antonucci, a chef born in Venice, who Dino imported from a restaurant in the Dominican Republic. He started his career at DDL Foodshow turning chickens on the rotisserie. So if I have to thank whoever creates these connections for one thing and one thing only, besides the enormous privilege of working with Dino, it was the introduction to Francesco, the only partner that I've ever had. We went on to work together for almost twenty years.

5

THE DESIGNER AS RESTAURATEUR

When Francesco told me of his dream to open a Venetian restaurant called Remi (named for the oars in Venice) and asked me to help find investors, in a moment of madness I said: Why don't we do it ourselves? And we did. When we opened on Seventy-ninth Street[5] in 1987, I was a designer. This was not my business. My passion for food really started there, because it was also my restaurant. Francesco was extremely shy, so shy that he would refuse to come out of the kitchen. The first week we opened, I found myself standing in the front of the restaurant and greeting people, because shy is not a problem for me. I invited everybody I knew, and at that point, I knew a lot of people: "We're opening our restaurant, come on in, bring friends." I stood at the door with sleeves rolled up, greeting people and seating them; somehow I had an instinct for it. I wouldn't say I knew what I was doing, but I could make people comfortable.

I had defined myself as a restaurant designer because I wanted to do design. But as I moved ahead, the hospitality mentality kicked in. As I went from La Coupole to Club A to other restaurants I was doing at the time, I was acquiring more knowledge about the hospitality business. And I realized I have it in me. If I saw someone unhappy at a table, I would go over and easily fix the problem. It just came naturally to me. Maybe I was born to be a restaurateur. But that took me by surprise. You can't learn how to be hospitable, you have to feel it. You either have it or you don't. It's instinctive, like talent.

So a couple of weeks into Remi, I get a phone call from a very important food critic, who said, "Adam, I was in your restaurant." I said, "I know you were in the restaurant. I seated you." And she says: "I have to tell you that it was the closest I've ever had to a real Venetian meal. It's extraordinary. Francesco's food was exactly like being in Italy." And I said, "Well, it's very kind of you. I really appreciate..." and she says, "I'm not finished. Please tell him that if he continues to cook like this, he'll be out of business in a month."

"And why is that?" "Because he's cooking the way his mother taught him to cook. There's no salt. There's no garlic. There's no pepper. Americans have a very different taste palate. They are not used to these subtleties. They will think that the food is tasteless." And that night was the only time in our entire partnership that I was afraid it was going to dissolve, because I knew I had to sit down with Francesco and give him this message.

At that time, my palate was not sophisticated enough to know this. I'd always loved Francesco's food. Italian food was my formation. I wasn't an American yet. And I knew that in Northern Italy, very few people cook with garlic. For me, the message was not the problem. It was delivering the message to my partner, who at that time was working one hundred hours nonstop. So we sit down and I tell him. Francesco looks at me and says, "No problem. We put garlic. We put salt. It's not a problem."

And at that moment, I think I became a foodie. Because I knew I had to really taste the food and to

6

know what I tasted. Tastings with Francesco were always done in my presence, and he totally relied on my instinct to tell him what I liked. Remi became the place where I honed my palate as well as my craft as a restaurateur. I started understanding what it takes to actually run this restaurant, not just to design it. I was practicing instead of just preaching. That experience was totally formative and the moment where my craft was transformed into something unique, something that I could package, something that would define me.

Physically, I was opening the restaurant at 6 in the evening and sitting with my partner at midnight looking at the numbers, seeing what we did well and responding to people who were unhappy. I was cleaning the floors, I was stocking the service stations, I was operating the restaurant, really operating it. Gradually I earned the right to say to a client: "I'm a restaurateur. I've been in your shoes for eighteen years. We opened four restaurants ourselves. Our reputation and names and money were on the line."

What changed was that I could anticipate the operational problems and not just the aesthetic problems. I could incorporate all these details into a project from real experience, not just as a designer. That experience became a tremendous asset I could now bring to the table. Meaning that when I tell a client, "This works and this doesn't work," I'm not just saying it from an aesthetic standpoint, or because I don't feel like fitting a service station next to this column, or putting shades on the

windows, or recommending a lighting system where you can actually reach the bulbs to change them.

Every day running Remi made me a better designer. It was like adrenaline. I was totally excited about going there every evening. I was never tired. I was never not there. I was never not in a meeting with Francesco discussing how to make the restaurant better. Paradoxically, the most difficult thing for me in this whole process was designing the restaurant. If a restaurant is a portrait, Remi was the portrait of Francesco and me, and I was terrified of making a mistake. It's one thing when you're working for somebody else, but the design of Remi when we opened on Seventy-ninth Street was a struggle. But by the time we moved to Fifty-third Street,[6] everything came easier. We eventually opened three more Remis in Santa Monica, Tel Aviv, and Mexico City.

THE BUSINESSMAN DESIGNER

The reason I say that the most important moment in my formation as a restaurant designer was the day I operated my first restaurant, is because I see this as a business.

I don't just do a stage set and say, "Hey, whoever gets it, gets it." People come to me with a dream; sometimes with money that they've saved all their lives to realize their dream. My first responsibility is to make sure as best as I can that whatever dream I will deliver has a very good

7

chance of being successful. And I know how important it is to respect other peoples' investments and dreams. Return on investment is crucial; I know this viscerally because I have gone through it myself.

I don't tread lightly on anybody else's check. And I never have. I am very, very careful about that because it is part of who I am. So in that sense, how much can you push the design? I do not want my legacy to be someone who designs places that are absolutely spectacular but were all failures. I want my legacy to be someone who moved the business forward, pushed the boundaries, and created a track record of successful establishments. My reputation rests on being able to say that I designed Per Se, not for the first year and then it's gone, but over twenty years. I want to be able to say this establishment survived the test of time. It is timeless. It is appropriate now and will be appropriate in the future.

There has to be an equation of investment versus long-term impact. For example, the wine tower we did for Charlie Palmer's Aureole Las Vegas,[7] in 1999. There was a whole process we took ourselves through to realize why it made sense. I have no trouble convincing a client to spend money on ideas that are not just for show—ideas with staying power, ideas with the chance to become a classic. You might walk into Aureole the first time and say OMG this is crazy, but ten years from now people say: This is what defines the idea of this restaurant. This is what holds it together. You get the bang for your buck. The wine tower in Aureole could have sounded a little odd at the time, but eventually it became the definition of the place.

What I am interested in is portraying amazing projects that move the profession forward and create something important. When a chef or an owner comes to me, I ask him or her provocative questions. "Let's say if I had the ability to give you the key to any establishment in the world that reflects what you want to do, what would you choose?" The clients I like best are those who answer, "Well, there is no such establishment." And that's when I know I can create something really new. From that I can deduce where we're going with the project. If the answer is, "I want such and such," it's more difficult to dissuade them or to talk them into doing something else. There must be a starting point. And the starting point for me is to understand what makes you comfortable.

I really, really like clients who cannot express an idea in words. They want something original. And those are the ones who I ask to cook for me. First and foremost, I say, I want to see the food that you will serve in this restaurant. And then I go through my mental process of putting myself at the door of an establishment that serves that kind of food, imagining myself as a customer: What do I have to see and feel and touch that will set the stage for this particular kind of food? My clients have to speak to me first, whether they speak in symbols or they speak in cooking. Many times people ask me, "How do you do it?" I say, "I don't know how I do it, but I do it."

We deal with perceptions. For me, each restaurant or hotel is a book that speaks in different languages and

words. But it tells you a story. And ultimately you come to these establishments for the purpose of experiencing that chef's story. At the end of the day, you come to eat. I can't be talking to myself; I'm way too knowledgeable about this. This is what I do every single day. I study. I travel all the time, I have to be ahead of the curve. I can bring some of the innovations I see into my projects but I cannot do that to the point that nobody will get it. To me a successful restaurant is a full restaurant!

THE DEFINING PROJECTS

Unlike most of my colleagues in hospitality design, I'm a bit more difficult to define, because my philosophy is not based on the way I design, but rather what is appropriate for each project. When I wrap my mind around a project, each personality, each location, each business challenge, is a distinct style indicator. The results are custom-tailored, site-specific; a bespoke suit. Instead of comparing me to my colleagues, compare me to a custom tailor or, as I have said, to a portrait painter. Here are some landmark examples.

In the early '90s, my good friend and mentor George Lang, the legendary Hungarian restaurateur and owner of Café des Artistes, took over Gundel,[8] in Budapest, a restaurant that dates back to 1910. The building itself had been a restaurant since the late nineteenth century,

very much in the haute French style. Then, during the Communist era, when opulence was frowned upon, the building's interiors were totally stripped of their identity, its impoverished surfaces covered with the infamous Formica. We could not find any documentation of how the original restaurant looked. So I worked with a completely blind brief to bring Gundel back to its great days of glory, this time as a great Hungarian restaurant.

George and I thought it would be wonderful to re-create a Vienna Secession–style, very Otto Wagner, the late-nineteenth-century Austrian architect. This was a natural since Gundel's new owner, Ronald Lauder, who later opened the Neue Galerie in New York, was a major collector of Vienna Secession furniture and art. So I went ahead and prepared an exhaustive presentation of the design for Gundel in Vienna Secession style.

We took the designs to Budapest a few days before we were scheduled to present the project to the municipality. Because it was a big, historic moment, George arranged a dinner with the head of the Historical Preservation of Budapest. I found myself sitting next to this gentleman, who proceeds to tell me, quite incidentally, how much the Hungarians hate the Vienna Secession period. By mid-dinner, I found George, and told him: "We have a problem. We can't do our presentation. We will be completely screwed." So, suddenly, I became very ill and had to be sent back to New York; the meeting had to be postponed.

We went back to the drawing board and redid the presentation and eventually it was a resounding success.

9

Budapest is a magical city for me and George, Milton Glaser was involved as the graphic designer, so obviously all the stars were aligned, and the project was quite spectacular. And working with George and Milton, well, that's what we all aspire to do.

The importance of Spago[9] was twofold: one, it was my first project in Las Vegas. Second, I worked with Wolfgang Puck and Barbara Lazaroff, his wife at the time, and he was the first celebrity chef to come to Las Vegas and open a major restaurant not in a hotel or casino. It was at the Forum Shops at Caesars and it was pretty massive. Spago was a turning point in the history of Las Vegas and what celebrity chefs could bring to the table. Suddenly, the city that put such high premium on entertainment and fantasy realized that food and restaurants could be part of the draw.

Food in the early days of Las Vegas was the all-you-can-eat-buffet for a dollar. Food was just fuel to keep people going; they wanted you to spend as little time as possible eating because it took time away from the tables. There was always an entertainment component that goes back to Frank Sinatra and the Rat Pack, there were always showgirls, but historically, gaming was what drove the city. Today, the entire economic composition of Las Vegas has changed: gaming is estimated at less than 40 percent of total revenue; the rest comes from hotels, entertainment, and restaurants. Restaurants and celebrity chefs are now a required element.

Wolfgang and Barbara's brief to me about the new restaurant was something like "Design it as if we had had the money to do it right at Spago Los Angeles!" All of Wolf's restaurants before this were small and of different styles. But now, his California cuisine in Las Vegas had to be served in a dramatic and theatrical setting. I clearly remember the opening day. Wolfgang was very nervous and pacing around. It's something that I learned about him through the years that we worked together: he is always very concerned with every detail and he never takes anything for granted. And that's what makes him who he is.

Wolfgang Puck does not sit back and send his people to open restaurants. He's there in person, on the firing line. At the time, this was 1993, he was very well known in California, but not in Las Vegas. Spago Las Vegas became their most successful restaurant. It was a huge hit, due to the team of people and the chefs. But what they did, which was totally admirable, was to cater completely to the locals. They made the restaurant a local place, and locals support it through thick and thin.

But for me, this was the first time I worked in Las Vegas, and I completely fell in love with it. I saw its potential to become the most important design laboratory in the country. It's a place where you must blow away the competition; people put a super premium on entertainment and design, and they have the money to support it. You have all the ingredients for work that goes beyond spectacular; it could be extraordinary. The world changes so fast, and as the competition becomes more and more sophisticated, you must reinvent yourself to stay ahead. So it's a dream place for a designer. The commissions are

10

there, the money's there, the opportunities are there. You can be immensely talented but accomplish nothing if you are working in a black hole where people are afraid of every idea you have: "We can't afford it, it's too risky."

In Las Vegas, risk is the brief. How big can you dream? How can I do something on my property that people will come and say, "OOHHHHH." It was this thinking that led me to the innovation at Aureole* six years after Spago, and that became the next level of madness in Vegas.

Maybe I had Las Vegas on my mind when Sirio Maccioni brought me to see the new space for Le Cirque[10] in 1996, because I believe that with a little bit of chutzpah, you can have fun anywhere. I'd met Sirio years before at the original Le Cirque. I was having dinner with some Italians, obviously he, too, thought I was Italian, and asked: "So you're a designer? Can you take this column out?" I said, "I can't take it out, but I can try to make it disappear." This was the start of our relationship. So by the time we got to Le Cirque 2000, I had already worked on the original Le Cirque, I designed Osteria del Circo, we had worked on several projects, and we were quite comfortable together.

So Sirio takes me to see this space, saying he has to move Le Cirque because of union issues. It is the Villard Houses, designed in 1884 by McKim, Mead, & White. Stanford White! Designed originally as a private home, it was at one time the Archdiocese of New York. We walk inside and it's a mausoleum. Very, very heavy-handed, eighteenth-century, over-decorated and over-ornate interior. And to boot, you cannot touch it. Landmarked

interiors means that the public has the right to walk through the place and behold the original interior.

I told Sirio, this was a big mistake. "What do you want me to do here?" He said, "We can't do anything." I said, "Well, there are two options. We fix up the place. Light it so people can see the beautiful details, and put in period furniture that works with these interiors; we create a museum. But I don't know if that ever translates into a lively, fun restaurant. Or, we fix everything, put in good lighting and treat it like the Italians treat their monuments: we restore it and then park a Ferrari in the courtyard." And Sirio looks at me and says, "And what would that do?" And I say, "Well, I think the new will make the old look a little bit less stodgy. And the old will make the new look a little bit less weird." And he says, "Do it!"

That was it. That was the discussion and that was the brief. And he never really looked at anything after that. I believed we had an interesting opportunity here. Le Cirque is the circus: The circus comes to town, pitches a tent, everything happens inside but it doesn't alter the piazza or wherever the tent is. It's an object within an object. We can do the same here. We'll pitch a tent inside the Villard House. We'll use things that are movable. Nothing will be fixed or permanent. It will be away from the walls. We'll do justice to a true circus! And that's exactly what we did. With just six months to finish it. Sometimes, the limitations and the restrictions, instead of shackles, became the catalysts to creativity.

The space inside the Villard Houses clearly needed a

11

shock to come alive, so I designed banquettes that were six feet high with red and yellow tassels. I remember being in Italy in the factory and the owner saying: "Are you out of your mind?" And the truth was when you looked at these pieces out of context they looked so meshuga, so over the top, so crazy, that at a certain point I was afraid: we're going to send this stuff and it won't work. All the furniture, every piece, was made in Italy. Typically, we will have prototypes made and shipped over. There was no time to test anything. I kept calling Sirio, sending him photographs. But the scale was a big issue, and it was just really a great act of courage on our part to gamble and just go ahead and commission all this work. You had to have a level of conviction that bordered on madness. I kept sending him pictures from the factory: "Sirio, look at this, what do you think?" And he said, "We better buy tickets, because they're going to kick us out of town."

Which meant go ahead, let's take the risk. Three days before the opening, I'm there hanging the drapery, all of it suspended on tension rods, not one screw into the wall. A really elegant woman walks in and asks if I can show her around. I give her the tour, explaining everything. As she's leaving, she tells me, "My name is Jennifer Raab." She was the head of the New York City Landmarks Preservation Commission (and is now the president of Hunter College). I had no idea. She said, "Well, you pulled it off. I have to tell you, like it or not, you pulled it off. You didn't overstep your boundaries."

Le Cirque did exactly what it was supposed to do. It

was a shock to the system and it worked. It was a very lively, very fun restaurant. People loved going there. They loved being in these palatial, gold-leafed rooms sitting on those very modern chairs. People want to go out because they want to have fun, enjoy a different experience, live for two hours in another world. With Sirio as the ringmaster you're going to his circus—a circus of people, of food, of life and color.

I've explained how at the same time the circus of Le Cirque was happening on Madison Avenue, across town, we were completing the restaurant for Jean-Georges Vongerichten in the Trump International Hotel on Central Park West. While Le Cirque was the very definition of flamboyant, Jean-Georges[11] had a totally different brief. It was designed to be the four-star restaurant it became; as sheer, refined, and elegant as the chef himself, luxuriously reflecting the light and calm of the Central Park it faces. The intent was to do something in the vein of the Four Seasons, which is such a complete classic that as it ages, it becomes even more beautiful and more interesting.

The design complemented the food and the style of service. There were infinite discussions about tableside service and guéridons, and how and when they should arrive. Cutting fresh herbs right at table. Brilliant. I designed the plates with lines, each a different pattern, so the food could be organized a bit differently, creating fresh and interesting mosaics of color and idea. Jean-Georges was really a very close collaboration that was totally food-centric.

12

We've done many hotels, but none has been as personal for me as the King David[12] in Jerusalem. Having grown up in Israel with a mother who lives in Jerusalem, we all try (consciously or subconsciously) to do something that will please our parents. So how better to make your mother proud than to redesign the most important hotel in the Middle East, that happens to be about fifteen minutes by bus from where she lives.

My relationship with the Federman family goes back some years when I worked with Ami Federman on the Dan Eilat, which was my first big hotel project. The King David was the crown jewel of the chain. And when it was time to renovate this iconic, world-class property, they turned to me. On our first meetings about the King David, I told them that I wanted the feeling to be inherently about Jerusalem. It had to be, considering the positioning of the hotel, overlooking the Old City. If anyone wants to see a portrait of an emotional Jerusalem, this is it. It's not the wailing wall; it's not about religion. It's about the majesty and the light of the city.

The first word that comes to mind is gold, like the light, not the metal. When the evening comes in Jerusalem, a city built of Jerusalem limestone, everything turns to gold. It is simply the most beautiful light you will ever see.

Part of the reason I'm so sensitive to lighting in everything I design is that I grew up in that golden light of Jerusalem. It became the guiding light of my persona. I wanted to capture it in the décor of the hotel. It is the city of David, after all. Majestic. Golden. How do you package

all that? It's really quite a responsibility. I did not want to change the DNA of the hotel, or its magnetic personality. Sitting in the lobby of the King David, you'll see a vibrant crossroads of the world, people coming and going. It's really a city square in the most beautiful sense. It was opened in 1931 and like all grand hotels of the period was a mix of period European and Egyptian-ish art deco, all wings and legs. Not pharaohs, but close. The renovation was a three-year process, opening in 1998. And recently in 2009, we returned to complete the last two floors, basically, another 150 rooms.

I was so humbled by the opportunity, and I am always pleased when I meet people who tell me: "We were in Jerusalem and we stayed at the King David. It was just wonderful." The King David is a wonderful place. It is not perfect. But I think that just because it's not perfect is what makes it perfect. But that's what you expect from a venerable historical landmark. You don't expect it to be like Beijing. This is Jerusalem.

Many years ago, I was teaching a class in restaurant design at the School of Visual Arts, and there was this guy in my class who was a little bit older and clearly not a student. One day I went over to him and asked who he was. "Well, I'm a chef," he said. That man was Thomas Keller, who, I think, was then cooking at Raoul's in New York, long before he went to Napa and became America's premier chef. We stayed in touch, and my wife Marnie and I went to The French Laundry on our honeymoon.

13

Sometime after that, in 1998, Thomas came to me saying he wanted to do his interpretation of a French bistro. That impulse gave birth to the first Bouchon, in Yountville. The relationship moved on until the day when Thomas told me: "We are opening a fine dining restaurant in New York, in the Time Warner Center, fourth floor." We went to see the building, which was under construction. The challenge was this: How do you take a charming restaurant in a beautiful, very laid-back bucolic setting, an auberge de campagne, really, and translate it into the fourth floor of a skyscraper on Columbus Circle? It seemed impossible to keep the same sense of authenticity.

From the beginning, there was Thomas's absolute insistence that whatever we did, it had to become a classic. But how do you present Thomas's ethos, his essential food, in an urban setting? So I followed him in the kitchen at The French Laundry, just watching the choreography from the moment the food comes out of the kitchen to how it arrives at the table. And the wine service, and flower arrangements, and how you clean silver in front of the guests, and how you bring it to the table. And the crispness of everything. The starch, the ironing. All that was something I was absorbing just to get an idea not just of how it works, but how it looks and how it interrelates. It was really like watching a very sophisticated ballet. The French Laundry creates a very fine dining experience with Thomas's sensibility, sense of style, and aura. And that of his fiancée, Laura Cunningham, who worked closely with me on all aesthetic decisions.

For me the question was how do you take The French Laundry out of its surroundings and set it in an entirely different environment, both in scale and location. How can you get the customer into the right mood when your approach is through an urban mall and not walking through an herb garden? Of course, it would have been possible to re-create a French country inn on the fourth floor of the Time Warner Center. A restaurant can be a set, after all. You can build it and people will come. It would be a little weird. A lot weird. But that was not the point. The point was that this was to be an urban New York reinterpretation of The French Laundry. Otherwise, it would not be authentic. Authenticity comes from many things. It's not just reproduction. So we had to craft a complicated set of rules to create a relationship, to insure that the two projects somehow belonged to each other, but at the same time felt dramatically different. Not easy.

One of the most interesting aspects of Per Se,[13] if you decode the design, is that it's an homage to classic French design, done in a very contemporary fashion. Just like Thomas's food. We took the classic proportions of French paneling, and instead of applying moldings, we carved channels into the paneling and recessed metal into them. Everything is an interpretation of classic French design, done in a twenty-first-century American language. The furniture is an unadorned contemporary take on truly classic French furniture. It's about proportions. French style is a code. You can reproduce it exactly as is, as

14

French décor. Or you can take the French décor and flip it over and create a modern version of it. Per Se became a pretty tight and specific design, but I think it's authentic for Thomas Keller. It really conveys his ethos and brand of hospitality and who he is and what he does. So again, it's a portrait of the New York side of his personality. It's a very complicated simplicity.

Around the time of the tenth anniversary of Restaurant Daniel,[14] Daniel Boulud asked me to redesign the restaurant. I knew Daniel from Le Cirque, of course, but we'd never worked together. His restaurant in the Mayfair Hotel was originally done by a French designer, Patrick Naggar, in a very dramatic, heavy-handed style that masked the architecture. I told him: "The bones of the place are lovely. But if we want to insert a contemporary life here, we have to strip everything down, paint it all one color so the interior looks more like an architectural model than an ornate decorated space."

What Daniel did not tell me right away was that the installation of the new design had to be completed in one month. I said, "Wait a second, this is not a set. There's a great deal of work to be done here." And he said: "It's got to happen overnight, because I'm going to Beijing for a month to open my restaurant at the Olympics and I am not closing this place down for more than thirty days." I told him that as long as he gave me enough time up front to design and order everything, have it custom made and ready in the warehouse, we'd organize the installation as a military operation. So I designed and ordered everything.

Daniel saw prototypes of furniture, drawings, of course, but nothing more.

What we agreed to—which was very clever on his part—is that every table would stay exactly where it was before. He didn't want to retrain his staff. This is a four-star operation. The waiters know their tables. They might not care about the décor, but they do care that the service station will be where they expect it to be. They care that they don't have to reinvent and reorganize, because Daniel is a well-orchestrated ballet, and every dancer knows his position. If you disturb this, you have to spend another month at least to train the service staff. But there was no training time. When they opened, they opened. Boom.

So he returned from Beijing and walked into the redone restaurant. "Hey, Daniel," I said. "Welcome home." He looked around: "Fantastic. Fantastic. I can't believe this is happening." Of course I had to have the confidence (and chutzpah) that I and my people could pull this off. But that's what we do. We went on to do a Bar Boulud in London and we're working on one in Boston, so the relationship continues.

An old friend, David Nicholls, corporate head of food and beverage for the Mandarin Oriental hotels, introduced me to Heston Blumenthal, the genius behind the three-star Michelin restaurant The Fat Duck in Bray, with the idea of opening a contemporary British brasserie at the Mandarin Oriental in London. Heston, who turned out to be very quirky and incredibly clever, had the idea to base the food

15

on historical sixteenth-century British cooking. He took me to the Lake District, way up north near Scotland, to visit the preeminent British food historian, Ivan Day. Day was a consultant to Hampton Court, so we went there too, to examine how the old kitchens were built.

Heston was transfixed by things like a watermelon, which, once cut open, would release live birds, and I was transfixed by an incredible rotisserie on a pulley system. Out of this research we created the contemporary take on all that for the restaurant Dinner[15] in London. That pulley was a spark, and I designed an incredibly sleek stainless steel, 2011-version to be the centerpiece in Dinner's open kitchen. I chose historically appropriate materials such as tooled leather, forged iron, and weathered wood, and designed a chandelier modeled on the windows of Westminster Abbey and glowing porcelain wall sconces, formed from sixteenth-century pudding molds. It's our version of a British brasserie with a meticulously researched menu that offers dishes like meat fruit, c. 1500, savoury porridge, c. 1660, and salamagundy, c. 1720.

KEEPING IT PERSONAL

The most important thing to know about my practice is that it is an intimate atelier built on the Italian model and not at all like a corporate American design firm. At peak times we have just sixteen people. I chose this profession because I want to design. Period. I want to be involved in every detail of every project. And once I exceed a certain number of people in the office, I find myself managing people and not working on the projects. I hire talented, passionate people who love the profession, who collaborate. Always. My senior people have been here sixteen years each. I've worked with Andrea Riecken, who now runs our office in Rome, for twenty-five years. People call this home, they spend a lot of hours here, and they contribute unselfishly.

I come here early in the morning for one reason, and that is to walk the studio and see where everyone is on their projects. They leave them out on their desks at night for me to review. I make my comments, I call meetings, I discuss things I'm not happy with, or very happy with. If I had to come in and organize manpower and go to meetings, I would not be in this business. If it was all about the money, I would be working on Wall Street. This is not an amazing money-making proposition. We make a living. I enjoy making a living and want to get up at six in the morning because I come here to look at designs that excite me.

Do we refuse projects? Of course we do. We have a big reputation, people know about us so we get a lot of phone calls and my biggest job is to decide where to put my energies. It really depends on two criteria: one, is the project interesting to us. Does it further our career? The second is the location. That is of cardinal importance because everybody in this office gets on an airplane and travels. I would simply not send them to a place they would not want to go! Ever.

Our practice is truly international—80 percent of our work has always been outside of the country. I don't want to see tired and unhappy people because they had to work in some secondary city in China. It's just not worth it. Travel is a lot of wear and tear. And you just don't want to put somebody on an airplane for ten hours to go somewhere they do not want to go. Marnie Tihany, who is our director of business development, has a list of cities where we will work. If someone calls about something not on the list, she has strict instructions to say "No!" unless it is something so extraordinary that we have to do it. It's a little game we play here: sometimes she'll call out a name of a city. And if everybody says "Yes!" we know we have to do the project!

Does anybody want to go to Venice? "Yesssss!". Nanjin would not get that response. People here are fighting to go to India on the Oberoi project. Why? Because you can work with the most incredible craftsmen in the world, the most unbelievable fabric weavers, the most incredible artists in small villages. It is complete magic. People go there and they are transformed; they come back full of ideas for the next project. Working in Korea, too, is so exciting because you see a young country where people are enamored with design; they respect quality. You know the project will come out better than you even designed it because they are so proud of their quality.

Typically we work on ten to twelve projects simultaneously, all in different phases. That's really how we can tackle so many projects with so few people, because at different times in the process, there are different requirements. Hotel projects last from three to five years, which is a challenge to keep the energy and the excitement going for so long. It requires juggling people, getting new people involved at different times. Restaurant projects are complicated and detailed and take about a year to complete.

Right now we're at work on two hotel projects: a redesign of the Beverly Hills Hotel and the Oberoi in New Delhi. We are designing a new Italian restaurant at the Broadmoor Hotel in Colorado Springs, a contemporary Viennese-style restaurant in Seoul, South Korea, and we're redesigning the main restaurant at the Cipriani Hotel in Venice, which I am trying to make contemporary Venetian without going overboard. What makes this office unique is the diversity of our projects. We roll with the punches and we like doing it all, from traditional to contemporary styles. Our clients do not come here to get Adam Tihany style, because there is no one Tihany style.

PER SE

Some years back, I was teaching a class in restaurant design at the School of Visual Arts in New York City. There was one person in my class who was not a typical student. He was a bit older and quite focused on the subject material. When I asked him why he was in the class, he responded, "If one day I want to build my own restaurant, I need to know what goes into it and how it happens." That man was Thomas Keller.

Over the years, Thomas and I developed a close friendship and did our first project, Bouchon, together in 1998. Per Se was one of our most complex collaborations. Building on the legacy of The French Laundry, the challenge behind Per Se was to translate the Napa Valley flagship's relaxed ambience and brand of hospitality to the fourth floor of a midtown Manhattan skyscraper.

I spent two years with Thomas, studying his modus operandi and sampling his food. Thomas is one of the best chefs in America—in fact he has won the distinguished title several times. His attention to detail is unsurpassed and he creates a feeling of warmth, complexity, elegance, and genuine hospitality through his food. Thomas's personal style and signature culinary attributes had to be embedded in the design of Per Se.

The most iconic element selected from The French Laundry to be brought to Per Se was the signature blue door. Establishing continuity in the experience, guests are greeted with this familiar feature upon arrival. The Per Se "door" functions as a symbol of the brand. The door does not open; instead it has two sliding glass panels on each side that open automatically when a guest approaches.

A contemporary interpretation of classic French décor is the primary motif of the interiors. This modern translation reflects the chef's American interpretation of contemporary French cuisine. Simultaneously, the aesthetic creates an elegant setting inspired by a Maison Particulière in Paris infused with a Napa Valley perfume. A sculptural reservation desk creates an architectural focal piece upon entrance to the dining room. A neutral color palette graces the room while natural materials like wood, stone, glass, and metal were used for the finishes. An open fireplace and walnut armchairs are intended to provide a feeling of warmth and comfort in the space. Traditional armchairs are contrasted and complemented by modern torchères at the dining tables. The finishes in the space are meticulous, from the luxurious fabrics to custom-designed carpet and furniture pieces. Together, the design creates harmony between tradition and modernity, California spirit in a New York City setting, and the warmth and sophistication of Per Se's acclaimed owner.

Pp. 38–39 **Entry and Lounge.** Pp. 40–41 **Bar and Lounge.** P. 42 **Bar – Detail.** P. 43 **Lounge - Detail.** Pp. 44–45 **Main Dining Room.** Pp. 46–47 **Main Dining Room and View of Central Park.**

Photography by Paul Warchol.

WESTIN CHOSUN

The Westin Chosun Seoul is South Korea's premier business destination. Built in 1914, the property has been a paramount piece of the capital's history and host to political dignitaries and key historical events. It was the first hotel to introduce Western hospitality to South Korea. As the previous site of the "rite of heaven," the hotel also features spectacular views of the Ancient Temple of Heaven, a relic that dates back over a thousand years and serves as a reminder of the city's rich history.

Seoul effortlessly blends the old and the new. Modern skyscrapers are set against temples, creating visual symbolism of the city's defining character. The hotel is an example of this unique combination of history and innovation. I was inspired by what some call the Korean "Harmony of Traditions," the perfect balance of modernity and tradition. Translating this concept into design resulted in the use of locally sourced materials such as wood, bronze, stone, and water. These design elements speak to the location of the property as well as leave the smallest carbon footprint possible, creating what I like to call eco-luxury with a contemporary edge.

Paneled in dark wood and complemented by cream-colored marble, the lobby is dramatic and enticing, featuring archlike architectural "gates" and prized artwork. Art was paramount in my design as the hotel's owner is an avid collector of Korean and international art, which is featured throughout the hotel. A prominent Henry Moore sculpture stands in the center of the lobby while other works from the owner's remarkable art collection are integrated throughout. Walking from the lobby to the ballroom, one can view an enormous Louise Bourgeois sculpture of a spider perched over the grass canopy.

To the left of the entrance, one will experience Payard, a tempting "pastry jewelry boutique" in collaboration with renowned pastry chef, François Payard.

Past the pastry boutique, The Circle Lounge is a relaxing bar and lounge overlooking the delightful gardens. Subtly transforming from a tea lounge during the day to a seductive wine bar at night, the lounge provides a comfortable and inviting atmosphere with custom furniture and lush materials such as velvet and leather.

The Ninth Gate Restaurant is located off the lobby and offers a singular fine-dining experience. Established in 1924, The Ninth Gate was Korea's first French restaurant and has a long legacy of culinary distinction. The restaurant is surrounded by history as it offers patrons rare views of The Ancient Temple of Heaven. My design celebrates the tangible history of the restaurant while creating an elegant contemporary contrast. Bronze gates and screens flanking the entrance of the restaurant highlight the views of the Temple outside. The walls are lined with silk and framed with dark oak wood trim and leather upholstery.

On the second floor of the hotel are the conference and meeting rooms. As the hotel is a popular choice for business travelers as well as social events and weddings, my design had to set the perfect backdrop for any type of event or gala. These rooms reflect a contemporary aesthetic with geometric lighting, lacquered woods, and a cream and chocolate brown palette. Some rooms feature expansive glass windows that look out onto the Ancient Temple of Heaven and feature interesting wood screens in intricate patterns.

Spanning the second and third floors is the eco-luxurious spa and fitness center. A dramatic entrance sets the tone with black paneled walls and a large, circular cutout of the ceiling. Three pieces of Francis Bacon artwork add a splash of red to the walls. Inside the spa, there are several areas set aside to partake in traditional Korean water rituals. The futuristic swimming pool makes an impact flanked by large white columns accented with backlit glass, exquisite blue mosaics, and an expansive skylight.

On the lower levels of the hotel are Aria and Vecchia e Nuovo, two restaurants that offer different dining experiences. Aria is the hotel's contemporary, self-service venue and features avant-garde architectural features, state of the art lighting design, and modern

finishes in stone and metal. Vecchia e Nuovo is connected to the lobby by a monumental staircase and echos the modern, architectural features of Aria but integrates a warmer color palette of the lobby above through the furniture and details. As the hotel's signature Italian café, the restaurant serves light and traditional Italian fare from afternoon to night.

A spectacular celebration of Korean tradition and modern luxury, the Westin Chosun provides a first-class hospitality experience through contemporary interiors, exquisite finishes, and modern amenities.

Photography: Nacàsa & Partners, Inc.

AT.MOSPHERE

At.mosphere is a restaurant and lounge unlike any other. Located in the Burj Khalifa, the world's tallest skyscraper, the venue is perched on the 122nd floor, thus making it the highest restaurant in the world. Creating the signature restaurant in this remarkable feat of engineering was the opportunity of a lifetime.

Guests would be either totally exhilarated or completely terrified by dining on the 122nd floor of a building. It was important to create an ambience that would afford guests luxurious comfort and a sense of intimacy to balance out the heaven-high views. Additionally, the restaurant had to reflect the local identity of Dubai and the Emirates while appealing to the diverse, global visitors the metropolis attracts.

Accessible only by a dedicated, high-speed elevator, guests experience the drama of At.mosphere from the minute the journey begins upward. The elevator doors open to a two-story, glass enclosed atrium and a cantilevered staircase, seemingly suspended in midair. Hovering above the staircase is a stunning sculptural installation of bronze rods by artist Carol Bove. Transforming the simple act of descending the stairs into a complete experience, the art installation was designed to align with the astrological configuration of the stars over Dubai on the inauguration day of the Burj Khalifa in 2010.

Once at the bottom of the stairs, guests can choose between entering the restaurant, a white-tablecloth, contemporary steakhouse, or going to the bar and lounge, Dubai's most exclusive destination to see and be seen. I imagined the interiors of an opulent vessel; a cocoonlike space where guests can enjoy the rush of adventure yet feel safe and protected at the same time. To accomplish this vision, I chose to clad the walls and ceilings of the restaurant and lounge in hand-polished wood. The curving walls arch around the venue, enveloping the space and complementing the floor to ceiling windows and dramatic views. Rich textures like velvet, silk, and leather in shades of amethyst and cocoa were used on the custom furniture throughout.

The restaurant features a dynamic exhibition kitchen where patrons can observe and experience the energy. Behind the open kitchen is an exquisite private dining room for twelve. World-class artwork was hand selected for the venue, including pieces by Yoshiaki Yuki, a contemporary Japanese artist.

The lounge rests on a marble-clad, elevated platform overlooking the sunken and lushly textured lounge furnishings, where patrons can enjoy the views from each seat. Like a super yacht soaring through space, At.mosphere continues to beckon guests into sumptuous luxury experienced at the top of the world.

Pp. 74–75 Burj Khalifa, Dubai. P. 76 Cantilevered Staircase. P. 77 Bronze Rod Sculpture by Carol Bove. Pp. 78–79 Bar and Lounge. Pp. 80–81 Lounge. Pp. 82–83 Main Dining Room and Display Kitchen. Pp. 84–85 Main Dining Room Detail. Art by Yoshiaki Yuki.

Photography by Eric Laignel.

THE LINE

Shangri La conjures images of paradise, eternal youth, and idyllic surroundings. Loosely inspired by this mythical Western vision, the Shangri La Hotel in Singapore is situated on a lush, fifteen-acre retreat set apart from the bustling urban streets and ritzy shopping areas of the city. Built over forty years ago, the property is intended to be an urban sanctuary, where hotel guests can escape the reality of city life and enjoy luxurious tranquility.

The Line is an all-day dining venue. Buffet-style dining is very popular in Asia. The restaurant's concept is market-driven self-service dining, offering guests a wealth of selections. With sixteen live cooking stations serving sixteen styles of cuisine, guests can choose from a diverse array of flavors throughout the day and night.

Departing from the traditional Asian palette of red and black and natural materials like wood and stone, I chose white Corian as the main building material. I intended to give the space the feeling of an IPod: a technological canvas on which to showcase the food. The food stations were conceived as islands, spread throughout the space to enable easy navigation for guests. Additionally, by placing the stations in various locations, I created intimate areas in an ambitious space with nearly four hundred seats. Connecting the islands, kitchens, and dining room together is The Line; orange-red illuminated glass boxes that zigzag along the walls and ceiling. The color of The Line is representative of fire, one of the elements of nature.

Beyond my intent to design a space that showcases the cuisine, I wanted to begin a meaningful philosophical dialogue on our relationship with food and its origins. Where does it come from? For example, if you think about where wine originates, the grapes grow from the rain, earth, and sunlight; all natural elements. Today it is easy for us to overlook our inherent connection to the earth through our food. In a restaurant like The Line, I felt it was worthwhile to inspire diners to think about food, the environment, and the connection between us. Bram Tihany created an ecological video installation in an impressionistic style, very much like a watercolor painting, that tells the story of how food is made. A functioning piece of artwork as well as an educational piece of inspiration, the video plays throughout the restaurant on strategically placed screens. Inspiring guests to remember our connection to the earth, the video complements the orange-red line running through the restaurant as a representation of the line of life connecting us all.

P. 86 Salad Station. Pp. 88-89 Main Dining Room. Pp. 90-91 Dining Room and Dessert Station. Pp. 92-93 Tandoori Station. Pp. 94, 95 Enclosed Terrace.

Photography by Sam Nugroho.

HMF*

The Breakers Hotel in Palm Beach, Florida, was built in 1896 by Henry Morrison Flagler, the visionary oil magnate, industrialist, and father of modern Florida. The stunning waterfront resort exemplifies classic luxury and is rich in history and tradition. At the resort, our team designed an exciting new dining and drinking destination named HMF, after the hotel's founder.

Located in the heart of the hotel, the restaurant would be located in the former Florentine Room, previously home to the award-winning L'Escalier Restaurant. The space was breathtaking and resembled a fourteenth-century palazzo that featured hand-painted ceilings and colonnades. Creating an inviting, modern restaurant and lounge in the room while being sensitive to its size, character, and architectural features would be our challenge as designers. We wanted to create a venue that would respect and enhance the old-world features but also transform the space into a contemporary concept that complemented the hotel's demographic and customer base.

A true believer in site-specific projects, I was inspired by the restaurant's location. Palm Beach is notorious for the glamorous cocktail culture of the 1950s and 1960s and the Breakers Hotel hosted many of these famous social gatherings. HMF would restore the timeless, golden-era sophistication by becoming a modern reinterpretation of that past era. Another integral piece of the design was inspired by the food and beverage concept to

be introduced. Traditionally, the Florentine Room had hosted evenings of fine dining, but the hotel's food and beverage team would be presenting a new "small plate," globally inspired concept, influencing our design to become a space that would foster sharing, conversation, and dynamic social interaction.

To encourage modern cocktail culture, undoubtedly the bars were a major point of emphasis in the design. Our team created two bars made of ribbon mahogany, one for cocktails and the other devoted purely to sushi. By constructing a large, open kitchen and installing two showcase food stations, we created energy, fluidity, and eye-catching displays. We intentionally accentuated the room's hand-painted ceilings by echoing the same jewel-tone palette throughout the fabrics and floor covering. As the space was quite large and had to feel conducive for conversation, custom furniture was designed and placed strategically throughout the room. Oversized lighting complements the furniture pieces by providing shades of intimacy over the strategically placed vignettes. Finally, the main focal piece at HMF is the illuminated, three-thousand-bottle wine cellar that proudly showcases the restaurant's extensive wine collection and is visible to anyone upon entrance into the room.

Photography by Eric Laignel.
*See disclaimer on page 245

DINNER

Dinner was an eventful collaboration between acclaimed British chef, Heston Blumenthal, and the renowned Mandarin Oriental Group. Ten years earlier, I had designed the MO Bar and Foliage Restaurant at the Mandarin Hyde Park London, and in 2010, I returned to the property to work with Chef Daniel Boulud on his London debut, Bar Boulud. David Nicholls, the corporate head of food and beverage and true mastermind of both collaborations, introduced me to Heston. We got to know each other over amazing food at his laid-back Hinds Head pub and an exquisite meal at the remarkable Fat Duck, both in Bray.

Heston had been refining an incredible food concept for years: contemporary dining inspired by the culinary traditions of sixteenth-century Britain. He thought the best way for me to understand this idea was to meet with the preeminent food historian, Ivan Day. As soon as I stepped into Ivan's home in the Lake District, I caught sight of a fully functioning, pulley-operated contraption, turning a piece of meat that would eventually end up on our plates. It was a spectacle to say the least: an original period roasting apparatus with a spit and all the trappings. Upon first glimpse, I knew I would incorporate it into my design.

To bring Heston's genius to life, I knew that choosing opulent or polished finishes would not be the right design decision. The space had to have a certain patina, an authentic look that would evoke the imagery of historic Britain while remaining a contemporary interpretation. To conjure the atmosphere of a period British manor, I opted for materials such as distressed leather, wrought iron, historically accurate brick, and smoked-oak wood floors and tables. I raised the floors in the dining room to allow guests views of beautiful Hyde Park, perhaps catching a glimpse of the Queen's Guard en route to Buckingham Palace. Every seat in the room has a view of Heston's active, open kitchen. A homage to Ivan Day's roasting machine, an ultra-modern, mechanized pulley anchors the space while rotating pineapples in front of a roaring fire.

DANIEL

The year 2008 was very memorable. It marked the thirty-year anniversary of my firm. It also marked the approach of the ten-year anniversary of Daniel, my friend Daniel Boulud's fine dining establishment. Daniel is one of the most well-known restaurants in NYC and in its tenure has become a fixture on the New York City restaurant scene. In that time, Daniel Boulud has invented his own modern version of French cuisine now known and loved by many.

Ten years of success on the Upper East Side demanded a fresh new vision for the space and Daniel wanted me to be the visionary. The restaurant is located in the old Mayfair Hotel, previously the same location as Le Cirque, the highly successful restaurant I designed with Sirio Maccioni years ago. My familiarity with the location and strong grasp of Daniel's constantly evolving food were the foundation of the new design of the space.

I created a dialogue between modern design elements and the neo-classical architecture much like Daniel creates a dialogue between traditional French food and contemporary reinterpretations. Large stacked rings of custom chandeliers hang from the eighteen-foot ceiling and highlight the artwork in the room. The art is fundamental to the overall design as it echoes other themes in the restaurant, such as the juxtaposition between tradition and modernity. Sleek, glass-encased light boxes showcase the traditional railings surrounding the dining room. Tree-branch-shaped wall sconces play on the restaurant's connection to the natural world and its seasonal cuisine. Framed by dramatic archways, the clean lines of the wine wall mingle with curved, velvet banquettes. By weaving an indigenous-artwork-inspired pattern of loosely connected dots throughout the restaurant, I connected all of the design elements together. The theme appears on the carpet, the chandeliers, and the fine china I designed in collaboration with Bernardaud, the famous French porcelain company. The design is a portrait of the chef, his creativity, and his modern playfulness with traditional cuisine.

Photography by Eric Laignel.

ONE & ONLY

I am absolutely in love with Cape Town, South Africa. It is one of the most fascinating cities I have experienced and has incredibly diverse geography, culture, and style. The One & Only Cape Town hotel was my first project in South Africa. It was an intriguing opportunity to create a luxurious, site-specific resort in one of the most unique locations in the world. In order to evoke the true spirit of Cape Town through my design, I grew to know the city intimately. In the four years I worked on the project, I lived the site, breathed the air, met the people, and absorbed the richness and variety the area had to offer. My local experiences produced a design vocabulary that embodied the natural surroundings and multilayered culture.

The One & Only Cape Town is nestled between Table Mountain, the newest wonder of the world, and the city's picturesque and popular Victoria and Alfred Waterfront. The breathtaking African landscape was an essential source of inspiration for the design of the hotel. The hotel's color palette includes the warm, muted shades of the savannahs, dark African woods, and earth-tone fabrics such as forest green and burgundy. To elicit the authentic feeling of Cape Town, all fabrics and materials were sourced from South African artisans while local artists were commissioned to create art for the hotel's rooms and public spaces. Tribal and contemporary artwork can be found throughout the property as well as signature art pieces I designed for specific locations.

Upon entering the resort, guests are greeted with a floor-to-ceiling view of Table Mountain; the ceiling is adorned with a custom chandelier. I was inspired by Cape Town's notorious winds while creating the piece. The chandelier is comprised of a series of glass twigs loosely arranged as if they had just been swept up by a gust of Cape Town wind inside the lobby. The local stone floors are accented with African-inspired inlaid rugs in the seating areas. Overscale floor lamps reduce the height of the ceilings, and bespoke furniture pieces create a warm and luxurious lobby and lounge.

To the left of the lobby is the three-story Wine Loft. Wine culture in South Africa is quickly gaining international acclaim. Climatic and topographic conditions simulate those of the old wine countries, producing some of the world's finest vintages. The Loft is a celebration of this local product, a discovery experience for guests, and a functional storage space for the hotel's five-thousand-bottle collection. Resembling a glass catwalk that you might find behind a stage, the Loft allows guests to explore up-and-coming South African boutique wines as well as the more prestigious brands.

Across from the Wine Loft is Nobu, the hotel's multi-level fine-dining venue. A global brand led by master chef Nobu Matsuhisha, the restaurant is known for its contemporary and creative Japanese cuisine. My design integrates Japanese influences while staying true to the restaurant's South African location, with ebony woods, warm tones, and signature features such as an origami-inspired staircase and a sweeping light fixture.

The hotel rooms and suites are divided into two distinct experiences intended to complement guest preferences and the fantastic geographical setting. The Marina Rise is the urban hotel, featuring clean lines, dark woods, and expansive balconies that capture the drama of the magnificent mountain and waterfront views. The Villa Suites are located on a manmade island set away from the main property, specifically intended to feel like a private escape. Exceptionally spacious, each suite has a private balcony or terrace offering direct waterway views. Suites feature African walnut wood, neutral fabrics with hints of color, and luxurious finishes.

The islands also contain some of the hotel amenities including the pools, cabanas, pool restaurants, and 13,000-square-foot spa. An oasis of serenity in the heart of the city, the spa design integrates traditional African patterns through cream marbles and wood screens with African motifs that provide privacy to relaxing guests.

The hotel's design speaks the language of Cape Town through the integration of a geographically inspired color palette, local cultures, traditions, and art. By sourcing local materials and working with local artists, I was able to stay true to the area's spirit while creating a unique style with a modern luxury undertone. The One & Only Cape Town remains one of my favorite projects to date in one of the most captivating places on the planet.

Photography: Mario Todeschini – pp. 132-149. Barbara Kraft – pp. 150-155

AUREOLE*

It was 1998 and Charlie Palmer was one of the hottest chefs in New York City. My wife Marnie and I used to frequent his former hub, Kitchen 22, in the Flatiron District, a favorite of chefs and foodie socialites. It was also the time when Las Vegas hotel owners were starting to showcase celebrity chefs as an added attraction to the mega casino's offerings. Charlie was approached by the developers and owners of the upcoming Mandalay Bay Hotel and recommended me for the design job.

I was introduced to one of the owners, Bill Richardson, on my first visit to the site. The hotel's construction was in full swing and the future restaurant space was an empty, cavernous loft. As we walked through the vast concrete cube, Bill told me their intent was to install a monumental staircase and to display his impressive wine collection somewhere in the new restaurant. I commented that there had to be a more imaginative way to capture this special room than dropping in a massive staircase. Additionally, the wine collection deserved a spectacular and dramatic treatment.

When asked about my vision, I couldn't give an exact answer. I told them I would sleep on it and get back to them in the morning. I stayed up until 2 a.m. sketching concepts, but nothing stuck. Unable to fall asleep, I turned on a late-night movie: *Mission Impossible*. The scene where Tom Cruise lunges around a vast, white space in a black harness came on. That was my aha moment. I imagined being in a restaurant with a towering wine cellar only accessible by harness.

That vision gave birth to the Aureole wine tower and the "wine angel," a new Las Vegas profession. The wine tower stands tall like a skyscraper in the middle of the space while resembling a portrait of the chef and his New York City roots. The sexy, four-story spectacle transforms the intimidating moment of selecting wine into a fun, theatrical event. Guests place orders and watch a "wine angel" leap 40 feet upward, pluck a bottle from the tower, and gracefully descend back to earth within a matter of seconds. It is one of the most enchanting hospitality experiences around. Mission accomplished.

Photography by Mark Ballogg.   *See disclaimer on page 245

APSLEY'S

The Lanesborough Hotel is one of London's most prized properties and is an officially registered British landmark. A stately building located in upscale Knightsbridge on Hyde Park Corner, it is a preferred destination of luxury travelers and affluent guests. Built in the nineteenth century, the property has elegant architectural features and is the quintessential embodiment of British tradition.

Over the years, I had stayed at The Lanesborough numerous times and was familiar with the hotel as well as with the general manager, Geoffrey Gelardi. Gelardi wanted to create a glamorous and contemporary experience that would service his guests through breakfast, lunch, and dinner. The new dining concept was named Apsley's, after the Apsley House, home of the Duke of Wellington and located across from The Lanesborough Hotel. Celebrity chef Heinz Beck would spearhead the kitchen with his award-winning Italian food. A grand space, The Conservatory was originally modeled after the royal Brighton Pavilion and featured a dramatic glass ceiling. My challenge was to transform the room into a modern venue that could seamlessly transition from day to night.

Emphasizing the splendor of the skylight, I hung three glamorous chandeliers from the rafters. Creating a focal point and a sense of intimacy, the chandeliers also set the mood as the restaurant transitions into the evening hours. I refreshed the interiors with location-appropriate, contemporary versions of Regency-style furnishings. Rich fabrics adorn the walls and gold-accented carpeting covers the floors. To further enhance the bespoke customer experience, I designed two temperature-controlled wine-tasting rooms. These rooms have glass walls that the customer can turn opaque with the flip of a switch thus creating a fully private wine cellar for special wine tastings. The restaurant's pièce de résistance is a "post-Renaissance" mural commissioned from artist Simon Casson, one of the most collected young artists of his generation. The artwork is an unorthodox interpretation of the "Old Masters" and embodies the spirit of the renovation.

Pp. 166-167 **Entrance to Main Dining Room.** Pp. 168-169 **Main Dining Room.** Pp. 170-171 **Mural by Simon Casson.** Pp. 172-173 **Dining Room - Detail.** Pp. 174-175 **Main Dining Room.**

Photography by Eric Laignel.

LE CIRQUE 2000

I met Sirio Maccioni years ago when a friend invited me for dinner at the legendary Le Cirque restaurant on East Sixty-fifth Street in Manhattan. It was the 1980s and Le Cirque was the epicenter of New York City social life. Fresh off the completion of night spot Club A, I was beginning to make a name for myself as a hot restaurant designer. Sirio and I struck up a conversation in Italian, and assuming I actually was Italian, he took a liking to me. He thought I was "simpatico."

In 1997, Sirio made plans to move Le Cirque to the Villard Houses at the New York Palace Hotel. The Villard Houses were a sacred space and would present quite the design challenge. Built in 1884, the Landmarks Preservation Commission designated the building and its interiors a historic landmark in 1968, making it nearly impossible to put one new nail into the wall. To make things worse, moving a beloved and cherished restaurant to a new location always carried the big risk of upsetting regulars who would inevitably be resistant to change.

Sirio was not wrong for mistaking me for an Italian the first time we met. He asked me what I thought of the landmark location. I said that we had two options. We could perfectly restore the space, put in great lighting, bring in authentic period furniture and turn it into a museum that nobody wants to eat in. Or, we do what the Italians do: we park a Ferrari in the middle so the old will be offset by the new, and the new will not look so new because of the old. There would be an amazing tension that will translate into energy and fun. He looked at me and said, "Do it." He never looked at the drawings.

Le Cirque 2000 was our most outrageous "circus" yet. In the bar, giant torches illuminated pre-Raphaelite murals by John La Farge. The neon bar tower was custom-made on site, with steel and neon loops low-slung over custom-designed armchairs. In the dining room, I designed seating that incorporated references to clown costumes, with pastel buttons running up the spine. Overlapping circles on the carpet imitated a spotlight in a circus ring. Draping the room in luxurious fabric, I created a glamorous tent, in line with the design aesthetic while also protecting the sacred walls of the space.

The press called the design visionary, inspiring, brilliant, and outrageous. Without using screws and nails we successfully "pitched" a freestanding circus tent of the future inside one of New York's most protected spaces. The granddaughter of Stanford White, the original architect of the Villard Houses, came for dinner one night and wrote an article in the *New York Times* in which she gave the design an enthusiastic seal of approval. Sirio and I went on to build five more restaurants together but Le Cirque 2000 will always remain our "Italian Job."

P. 176 **Entrance.** Pp. 178–179 **Madison Dining Room.** P. 180 **The Gold Room Bar and Lounge - Detail.** P. 181 **Madison Dining Room - Detail.** Pp. 182–183 **The RED Room.**

Photography by Peter Paige

BOCUSE

The Culinary Institute of America is widely regarded as the world's preeminent culinary college and has a legendary roster of alumni including many of the world's top chefs. I currently serve as the art director, advising the school on design and architectural issues and overseeing capital development projects. In 2012, the Institute made the decision to redesign the Escoffier restaurant, one of four dining facilities on its Hyde Park, New York, campus that are student-operated and open to the public.

The Escoffier was named after Auguste Escoffier, an early pioneer of French culinary arts, so the school's decision to rename the space Bocuse after Chef Paul Bocuse was fitting. A highly celebrated and influential chef, Bocuse is regarded for having a profound impact on the culinary industry as the creator of nouvelle cuisine, a departure from traditional French guidelines of cooking to the usage of local and seasonal ingredients.

Like Chef Bocuse and his cuisine, part of my design strategy was to take traditionally French architectural elements and give them a contemporary twist. The dual function of the space as restaurant and cutting-edge classroom was an additionally crucial element to the design. I wanted to create a space as realistic and current as possible that provides students with the best training ground conceivable. I thought the space should be accessible, open, and visible so we decided to take down the wall originally separating the dining rooms. The open concept injected energy and movement into the space, simultaneously providing the vital connection between the front and back of house. A sleek, new wine cave was installed that adds a gloss to the room while also functioning as an educational resource for the school's sommeliers and beverage professionals. I chose contemporary chandeliers, wainscoting, and geometric ceiling molding to speak to a classic French aesthetic in a modern key. To honor Chef Bocuse, custom-designed wall sconces were installed in the shape of chef toques topped with porcelain statuettes of him. In the private dining room, a commissioned painting of Bocuse and his nouvelle cuisine colleagues hangs under a statement chandelier, made of the chef's signature truffled soup terrine bowls. In the kitchen, a portrait of the chef is hung above the exit door, continually serving as a reminder for the students to strive for excellence.

Pp. 184-185 **Entry and Display Kitchen.** Pp. 186-187 **Main Dining Room.** P. 188 **Private Dining Room.** Art by Andrea Baruffi. P. 189 **Private Dining Room - Detail.** Pp. 190-191 **Display Kitchen.**

Photography by Eric Laignel.

GRAND ÉPERNAY

Ranked among the world's top cruise lines, Celebrity Cruises is known for modern luxury, first-class amenities, and impeccable service to travelers across the globe. The Celebrity Solstice line is Celebrity's most luxurious class of ships, the Solstice being the crown jewel of the fleet. With the intention of creating a vessel that would rival the world's top hotels and finest dining establishments, the team at Celebrity Solstice approached me to design the Grand Épernay, the main dining room and centerpiece of the ship.

The Grand Épernay is named for Épernay, a town on the Marne River that is considered the "Champagne capital" of France. A unifying theme in the design, I was inspired to create the feeling of being in a Champagne glass: a room evocative of old Hollywood glamour and the likes of Fred Astaire and Ginger Rogers. To achieve this aesthetic, there were unique design challenges I had to overcome. The restrictions in ship design are very different from designing a project on land. Movement and vibration are constant challenges, not to mention safety and function. A chandelier cannot simply be hung; it has to be specifically designed with limitations in mind.

The restaurant's size was considerable, commanding two stories with seating for over fourteen hundred guests. With the intention of changing the perception of the space, I designed flying buttresses that generate strong lines and make the space architectural in nature. The existing columns were clad in chrome, making them visually disappear into the backdrop of the restaurant. To play on the Champagne theme, I designed a custom chandelier composed of hand-blown glass spheres, reminiscent of bubbles. Each glass sphere was suspended on a straight pole making the fixture resistant to the movement of the ship. Rising two stories in the front of the room is a glass wine tower that displays over two thousand wine bottles. Inside, I designed a gyroscopic system that suspends each wine bottle separately, protecting and stabilizing the bottles while the ship sails. A grand glass staircase connects both floors of the dining area and adds to the sense of drama associated with a dashing ballroom. The final effect is a sophisticated dining space that expresses an atmosphere of celebration and old Hollywood glamour.

Pp. 192-193 **Main Dining Room.** Pp. 194–195 **Main Dining Room.** P. 196 **Wine Cellar.** P. 197 **Stairway - Detail.** Pp. 198-199 **Main Dining Room and Wine Cellar.**

Photography by Royal Caribbean Cruise Line.

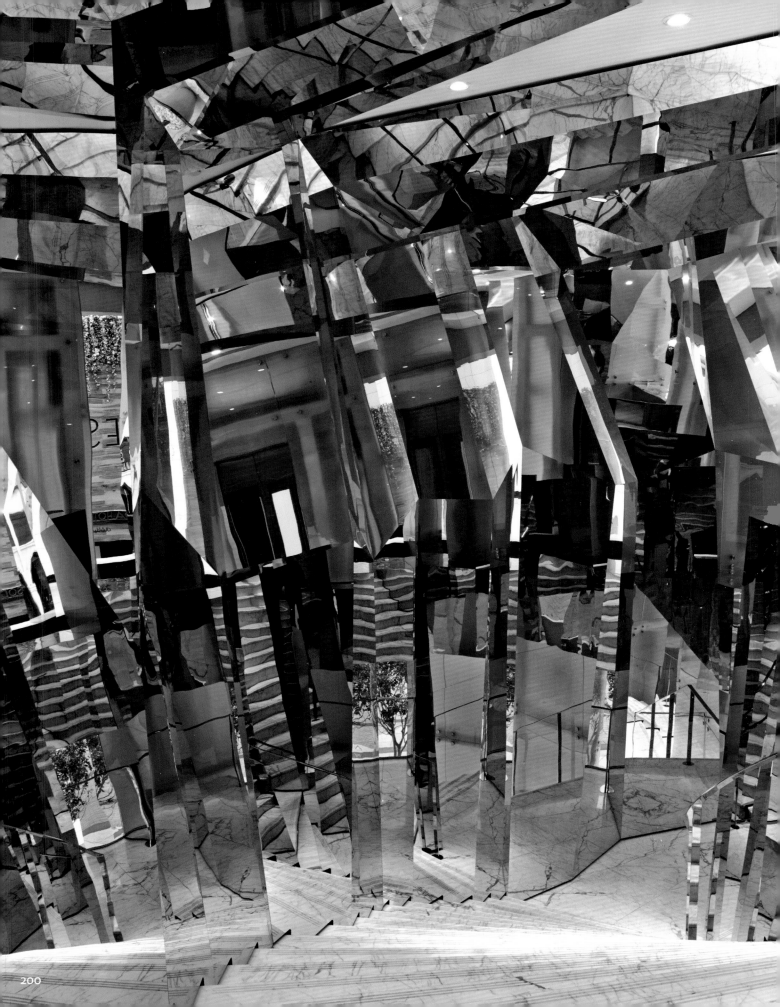

VERANDA

The Avenues is the largest shopping mall in Kuwait, covering over six miles and split into districts, much like a city. The covered mall functions as a city center and offers a central hub of social and commercial activity as well as a comfortable escape from the extreme weather. In Kuwait, shopping is a beloved activity. It is not uncommon to spend the entire day browsing and The Avenues offers shoppers an endless array of products and experiences to peruse.

The mall features the most desirable brands and high-end retailers including the prestigious Harvey Nichols, an international luxury lifestyle store with a prized reputation. In addition to the fashion retailing business, Harvey Nichols successfully transformed the top floors of all their stores into restaurants which have become popular destinations.

Veranda, on the balcony level of Harvey Nichols at The Avenues, is a modern and sophisticated restaurant, inspired by the concept of "dining on a cloud." I created an atmosphere that offers an upscale dining experience and a relaxing reprieve from a long day of shopping. The restaurant specializes in delicious farm-to-table "slow" food offerings, further emphasizing the pace and intention of the Veranda experience.

The bustling energy of the shopping center dissipates when entering the restaurant. From the "avenue" level, one arrives by ascending a custom-designed marble staircase that is enclosed by a dramatic, sculptural "canyon" of polished stainless steel, a strong and transformative arrival experience. Once at the top of the stairs, the tranquil dining room beckons with a nature-inspired color palette of creams, light woods, and fresh, green highlights of planted herbs and manicured trees. The walls and ceilings were designed to cradle the entire space with undulating dividers, reminiscent of soft cloud formations.

Gifted artist, Bram Tihany, created a custom landscape mural for the corridor connecting the store entrance to the restaurant. The mural depicts a series of oversized topiary sculptures of fashion accessories including a handbag, a stiletto shoe, and a pair of sunglasses.

A sanctuary of tranquility, Veranda is an oasis of rejuvenation and exquisite culinary delights inside Kuwait's most desirable shopping destination.

Pp. 200-203 Polished Stainless Steel at Stairway and Entrance. Pp. 204-205 Polished Stainless Steel at Reception Area. Art by Bram Tihany. Pp. 206-207 Main Dining Room. Art by Bram Tihany. Pp. 208-209 Main Dining Room. Pp. 210-211 Main Dining Room Balcony overlooking The Avenues concourse.

Photography by Eric Laignel.

MANDARIN ORIENTAL *

Las Vegas is one of the most important design laboratories in the United States. It is a city that places high value on unforgettable experiences, an open canvas for designers to create the most dramatic and theatrical environments imaginable. Designing the interiors of the Mandarin Oriental was a thrilling creative process that resulted in the creation of an unparalleled five-star luxury, non-gaming hotel.

The hotel is located in the City Center complex, the largest privately funded construction project in the history of the United States, created by an all-star team of architects and designers, with sustainability in mind. Mandarin Oriental is synonymous with luxury Asian hospitality and that was the driving force behind my concept. The Las Vegas property reflects the brand's Asian essence with Vegas-style, show-stopping charisma.

One enters the Mandarin Oriental through the intimate arrival lobby, designed in various shades of red and gold, featuring 7-foot clay sculptures by artist Jun Kaneko. Transported to the Sky Lobby on the twenty-second floor, elevators open to reveal the striking "gold bullion" wall, a recognizable symbol of prosperity and power in Asian culture.

The tranquil Tea Lounge and alluring MO Bar are to the right of the Sky Lobby. The Tea Lounge expresses a tailored, contemporary Asian aesthetic through lantern-inspired light fixtures, gold accents, and a crawling dragon featured in the floor covering. The sexy, low-lit MO Bar features wraparound views of the Vegas skyline and incorporates dark wood floors and jewel-toned armchairs.

Twist by Pierre Gagnaire, the hotel's fine-dining venue, is located across from the Tea Lounge. Pierre's contemporary interpretation of French cuisine inspired me to design a sophisticated, white-tablecloth venue with a touch of whimsy. The restaurant offers sweeping views of the Las Vegas Strip and showcases a dramatic glass staircase that leads to a dazzling wine loft. One of the restaurant's most striking features is arguably the lighting; three hundred gold globes floating in the air across the ceiling creating a soft, candlelit atmosphere.

Mozen Bistro, on the third floor, is the hotel's all-day dining destination. Featuring a neutral palette, the space is peaceful and rejuvenating. With light woods, creamy fabrics, and custom lighting that cast a warm glow, this venue offers a respite from the more dramatic mood of the hotel.

My concept behind the design of the guest rooms was to create spectacular personal sanctuaries. Generous amounts of natural light, rich textures, and clean, modern furnishings provide a majestic and tranquil oasis for each guest. The sleek bathroom is partially glass-enclosed affording daylight and a sense of spaciousness. For a more decadent escape, I designed an array of luxurious suites with distinctive styles. Ranging from a black-and-white contemporary retreat to an opulent suite referencing art deco style, each environment reflects an individual persona while maintaining the continuity of the Asian-inspired aesthetic throughout the rest of the property.

Known for fabulous spas, the Mandarin Oriental features a sprawling 30,000-square-foot haven of relaxation. Inspired by the exotic luxury of 1930's Shanghai, the spa features beautiful details, intricate geometric motifs, and luxurious embroidered silks. There are seventeen decadent treatment rooms, saunas, steam rooms, experience pools, a salon, and a dazzling hammam. The spa opens to the pool deck with two pools, Jacuzzis, poolside restaurants, and lavish, fully stocked cabanas.

From bespoke finishes to exotic influences, my design created a lavish hospitality experience amidst the unique energy of Las Vegas. The Hotel, Spa, and Twist restaurant were awarded the Forbes Five Star rating making it the only hotel in Las Vegas to be a triple Five Star winner in addition to holding the AAA Five Diamond Award title as well.

Photography: George Apostolidis - pp. 212-215, 217-243. Eric Laignel - p. 216

TWIST
BY PIERRE GAGNAIRE

ACKNOWLEDGMENTS

I wish to acknowledge the talented and dedicated designers who collaborated closely with me on the projects featured in this volume: Andrea Riecken, Rafael Alvarez, Carolyn Ament, Gisselle Ceniza, Rachel Cunha, Peter Lu, Bram Tihany, Agata Kowalska, Siriphot Manoch, and Alessia Genova.

Special thanks to Mirko Ilić, Dorothy Kalins, Charles Miers, David Morton, Ron Broadhurst, and Virginia Pizzi, who were instrumental in bringing this book to fruition.

Tihany practices interior design and does not perform architectural services. References made herein to "architecture" relate to various aspects of interior design that may have been incorporated into the overall design project.

In the states of Florida and Nevada, Adam D. Tihany acted as a design consultant to local architects.

*HMF (page 97) Adam D. Tihany acted as a design consultant to Peacock & Lewis Architects. *Aureole (page 157) Adam D. Tihany acted as a design consultant to Klai Juba Architects. *Mandarin Oriental (page 213) Adam D. Tihany acted as a design consultant to Adamson Associates Architects.

P. 244 **The Joule Hotel, Dallas – Presidential Suite – Shower Detail.** Photo by Eric Laignel. Pp. 246–247 **Hangar One Private Airport, Scottsdale, Arizona.** Photo by Paul Warchol. Pp. 248–249 **Aria Hotel, City Center, Las Vegas – Courtyard.** Photo by Eric Laignel. Pp. 250–251 **One & Only Ocean Club, Bahamas - King Room.** Photo by Barbara Kraft. P. 252 **Adam D. Tihany headshot.** Photo by Bill Hughes. Pp. 254–255 **Mandarin Oriental Landmark Hong Kong – Amber Restaurant.** Photo by Michael Weber. P. 256 **Aureole New York City – Detail. Art by Bram Tihany.** Photo by Eric Laignel.

"Problem solving is my inspiration."

Adam D. Tihany

Adam D. Tihany is widely regarded as one of the world's preeminent hospitality designers and an early pioneer of the restaurant design profession. After attending the Politecnico di Milano, Tihany apprenticed in renowned design firms in Italy. In 1978, Tihany established his own multidisciplinary New York studio. His practice began specializing in restaurant design with the creation of La Coupole, the first grand café in New York City in 1981. Tihany was one of the first designers to collaborate with celebrity chefs, having created multiple signature restaurants for highly acclaimed culinary stars such as Wolfgang Puck, Thomas Keller, Daniel Boulud, Charlie Palmer, Pierre Gagnaire, Jean-Georges Vongerichten, Heston Blumenthal, and Sirio Maccioni of Le Cirque fame.

His work in the hospitality field can be experienced in many luxury hotels around the globe: One & Only Cape Town resort in South Africa, the Mandarin Oriental Las Vegas, the Westin Chosun in Seoul, The Joule in Dallas, the King David Hotel in Jerusalem, The Oberoi Hotel in New Delhi, the Beverly Hills Hotel in Beverly Hills, Hotel Cipriani in Venice, The Breakers in Palm Beach, and The Broadmoor in Colorado Springs, to name a few. His studio perpetuates the philosophy that every project should be a living, relevant, and unique entity. Each project is custom-tailored to fit the vision of the client and is true to its location.

Tihany is an educator and lectures frequently in conferences and universities around the world. In 2011, he was appointed Art Director of the Culinary Institute of America. His outstanding contribution to the world of design has been recognized with numerous honors and awards including an honorary doctorate from the New York School of Interior Design and induction into the Interior Design Hall of Fame in 1991. Tihany was recognized by Who's Who in Food and Beverage in the United States by The James Beard Foundation in 1997, named *Bon Appetit*'s Designer of the Year in 2001, and awarded the prestigious Lawrence Israel Prize from the Fashion Institute of Technology in 2005. A recognized expert in luxury, Tihany frequently writes for international lifestyle, design, and travel magazines. His monograph, *Tihany Design*, was published by Monacelli Press in 1999, and his second book, *Tihany Style*, was published by Mondadori Electa in May 2004.